The Amazing Sparkleton Circus

By
William Rose

TABLE OF CONTENTS

Chapter One: Uncle Ballzwick

It was such a lovely sunny day on this quiet picturesque flower-filled street. A man humming a happy tune strolled up to a colorful house and gave the front door a quick knock. It soon opened and a sweet little old lady was standing there. "Yes? Can I help you?" she asked.

Henry Sparkleton, sweet guy but super goofy in his favorite polka dot pants and Hawaiian shirt, stood there smiling warmly at her. "Good afternoon madame! I represent the Luxo Dream Vacuum Cleaning System and I'm here to show you what an amazing cleaner this –"

She kicked him in the nuts.

"Yeowwweee! Holy cow grandma, I was just –" She slammed the door in his face. Henry couldn't believe it. "Hey, karma comes for all, you crazy wrinkle machine!" He cupped his nuts and started hobbling over to the house next door. "Man, I really need a better job."

He soon stumbled up to the front door of the second house and while still holding his balls with one hand, knocked with the other. It quickly opened and another little old lady was standing there.

"Good afternoon madam! My name is Henry Sparkleton and I'm here to show you what a wonderful new –"

"Why're you holding your balls?"

Henry looked down and noticed that his hand was still nuzzling his nuts. He quickly let go and reached it out to shake hers. "Oh sorry, nice to meet you."

She looked at the hand. "You were just holding your balls with that hand."

"Never mind the hand madame, I'm here to show you the revolutionary new way to keep your carpets clean for generations. I'm talking about the Luxo –"

"What do vacuum cleaners have to do with holding your balls?"

"I wasn't holding my balls! I was –"

She kicked him in the nuts and slapped the sunglasses off his face too. The glasses went flying through the air and landed out in the middle of the street. A huge truck soon drove over them.

Henry turned back around and glared at her. "Okay lady, that was not cool at –"

She slammed the door loudly.

Henry just stood there blinking incessantly like someone was blowing really hard in his face. "That's it. I need to go somewhere super spiritual and contemplate the mysteries of life while meditating on just how my life turned out to be such total crap."

# # #

Later that night down at the neighborhood bar that surprisingly enough was called 'Somewhere Super Spiritual', Henry was passed out face-down in a bowl of peanuts when a man came inside looking for him. The man headed straight for the bartender. "Excuse me, I'm looking for Henry Sparkleton. I heard I could usually find him here."

The bartender pointed to the end of the bar. "Where else would he be?"

The man nodded to the bartender and headed towards Henry. After reaching him, he just stood there wondering how Henry could breathe with his face completely surrounded by peanuts. He tapped Henry gently on the shoulder. "Mr. Sparkleton, I'd like to speak with you sir if you have a moment."

No response.

"It's of great importance to you."

Still no response.

"It's about an inheritance."

Henry popped his head up from the nuts, shells stuck in his

nose and hair.

The man continued, "Sir, my name is Mason Flugle and I represent the estate of your late uncle, the great Ballzwick Sparkleton."

"Ballzwick?"

"Yes sir. I believe he was an uncle on your mother's side. That doesn't ring a bell to you?"

Henry pulled a nutshell from his nose. "No and it totally would with such a cool name like Ballzwick."

"I see. That's a shame, you see he left his nephew, a Mr. Henry Sparkleton, a very nice inheritance in his will."

"Sweet Uncle Ballzwick?! For me?!"

The man smiled and pulled out some papers from his jacket pocket. "Yes, and I really think you're going to like it."

"Oh boy! Oh boy! Oh boy! What'd I get? Gold? Stocks? Bonds? Dare I even say..." he lowered his voice to a whisper, "...cash?" Super excited, he reached over and took a huge sip from a nearby drink that wasn't even his.

"Well to be precise sir, your uncle left you his beloved Sparkleton Circus."

Henry blew the drink out all over the bartender.

"A what?" Henry shouted.

"Damn it Henry!" the bartended blasted, "Will you stop doing that! Okay, the first few times were funny I'll admit it, but I'm running out of towels over here!"

Henry just ignored him. "What am I going to do with a circus?"

"Whatever you like sir."

Mason took a folder out from his briefcase. "Just sign these papers and it will all be yours."

Henry glanced at the papers. "Well, I suppose I could sell it. A circus has to be worth a lot of money, right? I mean, it is a good circus, isn't it?"

No answer.

"Isn't it?"

Still no answer.

"*Isn't it!?*"

"Well sir, at one time it was the greatest travelling circus of its kind."

"And now?"

"Well… now it seems that harder times had unfortunately befallen your uncle."

"Okay first off, if you're gonna be using words like befallen, I'll need to run home and get my World of Warcraft handbook."

"Sir, your uncle loved all the animals in his circus very dearly and look exceptional loving care of every one of them… but let's just say that between maxed-out loans and increasing pressure from the Tingle Brothers Circus trying to squeeze him out, the once legendary Sparkleton Circus has I'm sorry to say, seen its better days behind it."

"Excuse me," Henry said, pulling a nutshell out from his collar, "did you say maxed-out loans?"

"Yes, but you don't need to worry about those. Your uncle was able to pay them off. He had to or he'd lose the circus, but the payments kept him from properly keeping up with the necessary repairs and upkeep that a first-class traveling circus required. Since he was not about to sacrifice any comfort for the animals, he just stopped traveling and instead put on sporadic shows from their home base here in town."

"So, what's the bottom line?"

"Well, it pains me to tell you sir that the Great Sparkleton Circus has gone into severe decline."

Henry put his head all the way back down into the bowl of nuts.

The man smiled again and set the papers down next to him on the bar, "I'll just leave these with you sir." He then headed for the door but soon stopped and looked back at Henry. "And may I also say sir, there's something very special about this circus you should know about."

"What's that?" Henry asked mumbling through the nuts.

"All the acts in it are the very last of their kind. The very last anywhere, and the animals are all lovingly trained and cared for by the legendary Professor Puddin' Pottswaller and his daughter who are still with the circus.

Henry popped his head out from the nuts again. "Why do I know that name?"

"Well, aside from having the awesome name of Puddin' in it, the Pottswaller family is known far-and-wide for their love and great care of their animals. Something very hard to find in most circuses today. In fact, circuses themselves are hard to find today."

"Indeed. But I know I've heard that name from somewhere, I just can't seem to place it."

"The circus also features the last remaining members of the world-renowned Banzano Family Trapeze Extravaganza."

"I thought they were dead."

"Not yet. They're a little worse for wear though but I still think they have it in 'em. They were once the most spectacular daredevil trapeze act anywhere in the world."

"And now?"

No answer.

"And now!?"

"Now they've kind of gotten a little out of shape over the years. Most of them might need to go on a small diet or two, or seven."

"Big, are they?"

"And sweaty. Really, really sweaty."

Henry put his head back into the nuts.

"You sir of all people should appreciate saving something that's the last of its kind, seeing as you're one of the last traveling vacuum salesmen on the planet."

Henry popped his head back out again, "*The* last!" he said, then shoved it back in.

Mason headed for the door. "Take a look at the circus anyway. They're based downtown at the old Beacon Street warehouse. The address is right there on those papers." He opened the door and looked at Henry. "I believe you'll do the right thing Mr. Sparkleton. Goodbye." He stepped outside and was gone.

Henry just sat there motionless for a few moments with his face down in the nuts, then very slowly raised it up and smiled wide at the bartender. "Drinks for everyone on you Stinky! I'm gettin' a circus!"

"I've told you a hundred times, stop calling me Stinky!"

Everyone else cheered loudly for the free drinks.

"Sorry," Henry told the bartender with a sweet smile. "At least you're not dripping anymore."

Chapter Two: Fuzzbuns

The following morning inside his tiny apartment, Henry was sitting at a little round table in the middle of his kitchen with his head plowed into a bowl of dry cereal.

"Oh Stinky, what did you do to me last night?" he muffled through the flakes. "How late was I there?"

He felt a business card stuck to his forehead, peeled it off and read it. *"The Amazing Sparkleton Circus. Come one, come all to the most magical night of your life.* Sounds cool," he said with a smile as he brushed an amazing amount of cereal off his face. "Too bad I never had a chance to see it."

He got up from the table and headed straight for his bedroom... a wondrous land filled with endless stacks of comics, video games, toys, magic tricks and rubber turds he liked to use as gags at restaurants. He stepped inside and looked at it all proudly. "Not bad for a guy in his thirties." He opened the closet and looked into the mirror that was bolted to the back wall of it. "Well, Fuzzbuns, what should I wear today?"

He just stood there looking into the mirror for a minute, then slowly leaned off to the side and shouted down the hallway towards the kitchen, "Fuzzbuns? Are you there? You'd better not be in the mustard again!"

Henry's cat, DJ Fuzzbuns, was just licking the last drops of mustard off the side of a jar on the kitchen counter. He heard Henry but chose to ignore him like he always does.

Henry knew it too. "Dumb mustard-loving cat. He always looks like such a moron with his yellow tongue." Henry pulled out a spectacular Hawaiian shirt from the closet just as the cat came casually walking in licking its yellow cheeks.

"Guess what, Fuzzbuns? If all goes well today I'll be able to pay off the past-due rent, then move us out of this dump and get us a much nicer dump over on the east side."

The cat meowed and rubbed up against Henry's leg. Henry smiled and scratched its neck. "I mean how hard could it be to sell a circus right? I can just stop in over at that warehouse, take a quick look around, find out what's all included, then head over to that Flugle dude and arrange for the quickest sale possible."

Something on the floor of the closet suddenly caught the cat's eye. It pounced over to it and began playing with a piece of shiny ribbon.

Henry walked over to check it out. "What'cha got there, pal?" He reached underneath a stack of semi-finished 'Crossword Puzzles for Idiots' and pulled out a shoebox that had a sparkling metallic ribbon peeking out from under the lid. "Hey, I was wondering where this box went to." He looked at Fuzzbuns, "This was the box my aunt gave to my mother when I was a kid." He opened it. "I've never even looked in here yet. I always meant to but kept forgetting."

Little stacks of letters and assorted pictures all tied neatly with colorful bows were carefully placed inside. On top of them all was a single red feather and a handful of multi-colored carnival ribbons. He took out one of the pictures. It was of Henry as a little boy, standing between a jovial circus host and a beautiful white horse with a glorious red plume on its head. "Why don't I remember this?" he wondered aloud.

The cat took the quiet opportunity to sneak back into the kitchen and look for some more mustard, but Henry noticed it. He waited just until the cat was in the doorway of the kitchen, then loudly shouted... "You'd better not be going for the mustard again!"

The cat jumped three feet into the air and tore off running down the hall as fast as it could. Henry laughed contently and placed the letters back into the box. "That never gets old."

# # #

Stepping outside of his apartment a short time later, Henry walked right into the sour face of his unhappy landlord, Mr. Dousbagè who was just getting ready to knock on the door.

"Mr. Douchebag! So happy to see your lovely smiling face this morning!" Henry said as he blew right by him.

"That's Dousbagè, Sparkleton. It's French! I've told you that a hundred times, now where's my rent?"

"How fortuitous you happen to bring that up now Douchebag since I was just on my way to see about that right now."

"No kidding, where've I heard that before? Let's see..."

"No really, I've come into a little inheritance that I was just leaving to expound upon this very moment."

"Listen Sparkleton, I'm gonna expound a windsock from your nutsack if I don't get my money by the end of today! Got it?"

"Wow, why does the universe have it in for my nuts so bad?" Henry wondered a little too loudly as he climbed into his car and started the engine. A huge blast of smoke blew out from the tailpipe and completely covered Dousbagè in a thick cloud of exhaust. Henry leaned out the window, "Got it, Douchebag!" then pulled away with a loud squeal. It took several minutes before you could even see there was a human standing in the smoke.

Henry was giggling his buns off at it in the rearview mirror while simultaneously banging and bouncing all around the inside of his car from the totally blown shock absorbers. "I'm pretty sure this car might be due for a tune-up," he said, his voice shaking uncontrollably from the jolting. "Not positive but I should probably look into it."

The car backfired so loudly that people walking nearby, dove into bushes and leapt behind dumpsters thinking it was gunfire. Henry laughed, "That never gets old either."

He pulled out the business card from his shirt pocket. It took a while too because his head was constantly slamming into the roof. "Okay let's see now, the Beacon Street warehouse should be right up here somewhere." He glanced down the road and his face lit up. "Ah ha!" he exclaimed when he saw the joyful clown face plastered on a little metal sign signifying its location. He pulled into the small parking lot, grabbed a space right up front and tried to get out of the car but the door stuck, so he just climbed out the side window and headed straight for the main door of the building. A colorful sign was attached above it: *Beyond this realm are the makers of dreams and the purveyors of smiles.*

Henry looked at it and beamed like a wonder-filled child. "Cooooooool" he whispered, then slowly pushed open the door.

Chapter Three: Dwarf Dilemma

Henry stepped inside and found himself in a magical world filled with all things circus. There were colorful banners on the walls, glossy programs piled around, and stacks of popcorn tubs everywhere. Above the door was a massive poster featuring the Professor Pottswaller Animal Spectacular, the Mighty Mini Clown Act, and *'direct from Italy... the Banzano Family Trapeze Extravaganza!'*, all looking highly athletic, well-built and in tip-top shape.

"Wow, they look great," Henry mused just as the door to the main room in front of him flew open loudly and a humongous hairy beast of a man, Beppi Banzano, star flyer of the Banzano Family Trapeze Extravaganza was standing before him. He was huge too in his really tight, stretched-to-the-max, sweat-soaked, pink sparkling jumpsuit.

Henry screamed like a schoolgirl, and that scared Beppi who screamed like a schoolgirl. "Holy sheet! Who the hell are you?!" Beppi shouted.

"I'm the guy who has to change his undies now thanks very much! Who are you?" Henry asked completely surprised.

Beppi pointed up to the poster above the door.

"Are you a poster salesman?" Henry asked.

Beppi shook his head, "That'sa me flying through the air!"

Henry looked up at it again. "No it's not!"

"Yes it is!"

"The guy in that poster is fit and looks like a Mediterranean model. You're four-hundred pounds and look like Stromboli and a gay sumo had a kid then then rolled it in a bag of Shrek."

"Kissa my ass! What are you doing here?"

"I'm the new owner of this circus."

"You can call me papa," Beppi said giving Henry a nice big hug.

Henry smiled. "Actually, the reason for my visit today is because my great uncle was Ballzw—"

A loud bang from the room behind Beppi scared them both as a dwarf clown crashed loudly into a huge stack of metal buckets. It was the main room where the circus rehearsed and performed for local crowds. It had a backstage area separated by big black curtains, and numerous rows of bleachers set up out front for people to watch.

Beppi and Henry quickly ran inside and saw the clown sprawled out on the floor amongst the bleachers.

The clown saw Betto approaching and quickly pointed to a horse that was standing in front of him. "He kicked me!" the dwarf shouted in the cutest little voice you ever heard.

Tina Pottswaller, daughter of animal trainer Professor Puddin' Pottswaller, quickly came to the horse's rescue. "Oh Hugo, you probably just scared him that's all."

"I was just walking by!"

The horse seemed to actually be grinning a little.

The clown pointed at the horse. "Look at him! He's laughing at me!"

"Caesar wouldn't hurt a fly and you know it. He's just happy to see you."

"No, he's not! That's the same look he had when he farted in the clown car just as I was about to get inside!"

A few random crew members could be heard laughing from the shadows.

"See! Even *they* know it!"

"Don't you think you're exaggerating just a little?" Tina asked.

"Exaggerating? I couldn't get out of that car fast enough!"

More people in the room were now laughing.

"And the door was locked!" He pointed to the horse again... "And *he* did it!!!"

The entire room was now cracking up.

"A horse can't lock a door Hugo," she said gently taking the horse's reigns and leading it to the backstage area. However just before the horse had completely turned the corner, it looked back around at the clown and definitely smiled.

The clown saw it and looked like he was about to explode.

Beppi told Henry, "Justa forget about that little guy. He alwaysa thinks the animals have it in for him."

Henry smiled and held out his hand. "I'm Henry. Looks like a really fun place you have here."

"You'd think so wouldn't you," Beppi told him shaking his hand. "I'ma Beppi."

"What's a beppi?"

"No, my name isa Beppi."

"Oh, I see. Nice to meet you."

"Beppi pointed to the ringmaster. "That'sa Fred Baxter. He'sa the Master of Ceremony here. Everyone calls him Ted Baxter because he sounds justa like that goofy news reporter from the old Mary Tyler Moore TV show."

"Oh yeah, I've seen the old reruns. They were funny," Henry told him.

"Fred alwaysa talks in a deep old-school broadcaster's voice all the time. It'sa hilarious! Everything that comes out of his mouth sounds like he's about to take caller twelve to win monster truck tickets on some radio station." Beppi pointed over to Tina who was now busy brushing the horse's tail. "That'sa Miss Pottswaller. Her father isa the legendary animal trainer Professor Puddin' Pottswaller. No one takes better care of their animals thana that family."

"Is the professor still part of the circus?" Henry asked.

"Sort of. He's around here all the time, and is a real sweet guy too, but nuttier than squirrel turds under an acorn tree. His daughter runsa the act now."

Beppi pointed to the dwarf clown in the corner. "That little guy over there is Hugo, the Mighty Mini Clown Act. He'sa the resident midge."

"I think they like to be called little people," Henry told him.

"Nah, that's just a conspiracy theory."

"Well, he seems feisty."

"Oh, he's a real pain in the ass! But that's only because the animals are always messing with him."

Henry slid a nearby stool over to him and sat down, starting to get really engrossed.

Beppi continued. "Not only do all the animals think it'sa totally hilarious to make each other mess up during their performances, but they also love terrorizing the clown every chance they get. Like whena the monkey would slap the horse's butt and make it look like it wasa the clown's fault, the horse would then kicka the clown into the next time zone."

Henry started applauding. "That's brilliant!"

"Yeah, but the clown would come back really mad and put water in the bucket instead of confetti. Then he'd throw it at the horse, but he'd missa the horse and hit me instead!"

"How was my uncle able to keep all of this together?"

"Who's your uncle?"

"Oh, that's right, I never told you yet. As I was saying before, my name's Henry Sparkleton. I'm the nephew of Ballzwick Sparkleton."

The room instantly fell silent.

"I recently inherited this circus and just came here to look things over a bit because I actually plan on se—"

"You've come!" Tina exclaimed.

"Excuse me?"

"We just knew you'd show up sooner or later! Uncle Ballzwick told us he had a plan to continue the circus, but we didn't know exactly what he had planned."

"Uncle Ballzwick?"

"Oh, we all called him that. We were just like family to him. Truly a sweet man," she smiled warmly, "and now you're here to take things over and make everything okay again."

"Well, ahhhh..." he looked down at his shoes, "I'm not quite sure what to say but, I... oh boy... I really hate to tell you guys this, but I came here to sell the circus."

"What???!!!" everyone in the entire room shrieked at the same time. Henry covered his face with his arms to shield it from the shockwave.

"I'm sorry! But what do I know about running a circus?"

"We cana show you," Beppi told him.

"That's right!" Tina said. "Everyone here can teach you. We can all show you the ropes and get you up to speed on what to do."

"But I hate ropes, and speeding makes my car fall apart."

"How about this," Tina said, "we were just ready to start rehearsal when you came in. Why don't we just put on a full show for you right now, that way you can see how special this circus really is?"

Henry looked at his watch. "Well, I was gonna try and sell a few vacuums, knock on some doors, maybe get kicked in the nuts a few times before lunch, but I guess I can stay for a while."

"Great!" She clapped her hands to gather the troops. "Okay everyone, listen up!" she looked back at Henry and quietly mouthed, "Maybe get kicked in the nuts a few times before lunch?"

"Old ladies really have it in for my balls," he told her rather loudly.

She laughed and continued addressing the cast. "Alright, we've got one chance here to show Henry what this circus is all about, so let's do a good job!" She looked around the room, cupped her mouth and yelled out… "Daddy? Where are you?"

"Right here honey," a sweet voice was quickly heard. Out from the shadows walked Professor Puddin' Pottswaller, legendary animal trainer known throughout the business for the exceptional care he always gave to all his animals. He was five-foot tall and wore an old-school safari outfit complete with huge, oversized pith helmet. He had a funny little voice, was cute as a button, looked just like Elmer Fudd and was totally bat-shit crazy. He walked up to Beppi. "Here I am dear."

"No daddy, over here." Tina shouted from across the room.

He turned around and headed towards the voice. "Oh, there you are. Sorry sweetheart."

"Hi daddy, okay this is important so please try to listen. I know that occasionally you're in the here-and-now for just moments at a time, so I'm really hoping now is one of those moments because –"

"Do rubber chickens think *people* are funny?" he asked out of nowhere.

"What? Daddy listen, there's a man here who says he's the nephew of Uncle Ballzwick and wants to sell the circus," she gently took the professor him by his arm and guided him to the backstage area, "so I think it would be best if you just waited for me right here." She led him over to a nearby couch. "You can lay down here daddy till I get back and then I'll fix your lunch, okay?"

"Okay. By the way, I think a good name for a German bra shop would totally be Stoppinzeefloppin."

She smiled, lifted his helmet and kissed the top of his bald head. "I love you daddy."

Suddenly in his eyes she could see that he was really there for a moment. "I love you too sweetheart," he said.

"I'll be back as soon as I can, okay daddy?"

"Okay honey."

She smiled again and took off running back to the performance area.

Out in front by the bleachers, Henry giggled with anticipation as he grabbed a good seat up close to get the best view possible. And in no time at all, the room went dark, and the hum of loudspeakers quickly filled the air. The show was about to begin.

Chapter Four: Now That's Entertainment!

"Ladies and gentlemen, boys and girls of all ages, welcome to the most magical night of your life! Welcome to the Amazing Sparkleton Circus!" the Ringmaster's voice echoed throughout the room.

Colorful lights quickly splashed across everything, and joyful music filled the room as the performers began walking out from the backstage area, one-by-one.

First out was Tina, walking gently next to Pagoda the elephant.

Behind the elephant came the dazzling Banzano Family Trapeze Extravaganza, which was really now only Beppi, his brother Giuseppe, and their grandmother who everyone just called Granny Whiskers because she had reeeeally long gray mustache hairs that hung down her face like an old Chinese philosopher.

Behind the Banzanos came the dwarf clown, walking backwards and flipping off the horse who was still waiting in the wings watching him.

Next out was the horse... grinning maliciously at the clown.

On top of the horse was a cute little dog doing back-flips.

Behind the horse walked Chester the monkey, wearing lederhosen, eating peanuts and nailing the dog with the shells who kept leaping all over the horse's back trying to dodge them. It wasn't part of the act. The monkey just loved doing that.

While everyone gathered in the center ring to wave at the audience, the clown took the opportunity to sneak off and grab an orange off a nearby table. When he thought no one was looking, he hurled it at the horse, but it missed and hit Beppi in the back of the head instead, causing Beppi to stagger forwards and crash into the monkey who quickly turned around and slapped the shit out of Beppi's face.

The ringmaster obviously wasn't paying attention. "What a happy sight, right folks?"

Beppi screamed and ran from the ring, but the monkey quickly began chasing after him.

Tina saw it and instantly ran after the monkey who was right on Beppi's ass.

The oblivious ringmaster continued. "Isn't this a magical day everyone?"

Beppi soon saw a large tub of water nearby and quickly dove into it.

The monkey reached the tub as well and was just about to grab Beppi's hairy buttsteak when Tina arrived just in time and snatched the monkey away right at the last second. But as Tina was swinging the monkey away from the tub, the monkey reached out its hand and splashed some of the water on the horse who was standing nearby.

The horse looked at the monkey.

The monkey pointed to Beppi.

Beppi, thinking everything was safe now, rose up from the tub where the horse was waiting for him. It immediately kicked him all the way across the room to where Professor Pottswaller was laying on the couch. The Professor looked down at him spread out all over the ground. "Wow honey, you really let yourself go!"

"It's me you moron! I've just been kicked by your horsey again!"

The ringmaster began singing. "*Circus is forever, circus is love!*"

"Shut up Fred!!!" the entire room yelled at the same time.

"Will someone please turn the lights back on!" Tina shouted.

Soon the room lit up brightly and everyone just fell silent, nervously looking over at Henry who was sitting there with his mouth wide open, staring in complete and utter disbelief.

Tina tried to quickly smooth things over. "This... doesn't usually happen."

"Bullsheet! It happens all the time!" Betto blasted out.

But before Tina could even respond, Henry raised his hand. "Well, I have to tell you guys that I really…"

Everyone's eyes widened as they prepared for the worst.

"…really…"

Tina gulped hard.

"Loved it! Is there any way you guys can do that every night?"

"What?!" Tina asked, thoroughly amazed. "You want us to purposely do that every night?"

"Yes! It was entertaining! I almost peed my pants!"

"But Henry, we're professionals," she said looking around the room, "well most of us are, and we can't just smack each other around every night."

"Yesa we can," Beppi told her.

"Zip it Beppi. Anyway, I know we could put on a first-class circus if we just had a little more time."

"But will it make any profit at all?" Henry asked.

"If we can bring it to its full potential, then yes, it can," she told him.

"Okay, you guys do whatever you have to do to get this circus together and I'm gonna to go see that lawyer for my uncle's estate about getting us an advance on some of those profits. We'll need some cash to get this whole thing fixed up, right?"

Tina walked over and gave him a big hug. "Thank you for not selling it. I promise you we'll work hard."

He smiled sweetly at her. He liked her.

Chapter Five: Fartsnacker

Outside the building, Henry was totally energized and ran excitedly to his car, hoping the door would open this time… and it did! But it immediately fell off the hinges and crashed to the ground.

"Oh great! How am I supposed to keep a circus running when I can't even keep a door attached to my car?"

He picked it up, opened the rear door, tossed it in, slammed the door and it too fell off the hinges crashing to the ground. He just ignored it and climbed into his sort-of car. He started the engine, and it immediately backfired loudly sending two more people diving into nearby bushes.

"Nice," he said with a smile, immediately feeling better. He squealed away from the parking space, barely remaining inside as he whipped out into the street.

He soon came to a stop at a nearby traffic light where the people in the car next to him looked over and burst out laughing.

As Henry was looking around the car for something to quickly throw at them, a stray dog walked up and climbed into the wide-open backseat. It just sat down and stared at Henry.

Henry turned around and smiled at it. "Hiya buddy. You might wanna hang onto your balls, this thing moves."

The light turned green, and Henry immediately floored it, completely consuming the car next to him in thick black smoke.

While Henry and the dog flew down the street, Henry cranked up the radio and laughed like a little kid as the shitty shock absorbers bounced them both all over the inside of the car.

But that wasn't all…

"You ready for hyper-speed pal?"

The dog barked happily.

"Watch this." Henry hung on tight then floored the gas pedal, but the car died out instead. It slowly came to a complete stop then backfired one last time.

"Oh come on! I was almost there!" he shouted as he stepped easily out from the car. He walked around to the front, lifted the hood where smoke immediately poured out from the engine. He closed the hood and walked back to the dog. "Well buddy, looks we're hoofin' it the rest of the way."

The dog happily climbed out from the car. Henry gave it a nice scratch and checked for a collar. There wasn't one.

"No home, huh boy? Well, you got one now. I'm Henry, and I think I'll call you Fartsnacker."

The dog barked.

"Why? Because I always wanted a dog named Fartsnacker that's why. It's cute! Either that or Fartknuckled Dickosaurus but that's way too long for a name tag."

The dog barked again.

"I knew you'd agree. Thanks, pal. We're gonna get along great."

As they started walking down the street together, Henry pointed up the road ahead. "Should be just around that corner." He looked down at the dog and laughed... "Wait till you meet DJ Fuzzbuns. He's gonna shit a mustard cannonball when he sees you!"

# # #

In a small nondescript office building that was indeed just around the corner, Mason Flugle was busy talking on the phone. A takeout container filled with a roast beef sandwich sat on his desk.

"As much as I'd love to see it happen, I really don't think he can save the circus. He's a likable enough guy and all, but I think he's totally crazy." He put his feet up on the desk. "What? No, I don't think he wants to keep it going. Probably hasn't even gone down there yet. In fact, if I see him anytime soon at all, I think it'll be a complete miracle."

The door to his office kicked open loudly and Henry jumped inside. "Hiya Fartknuckled Dickosaurus!!!"

Mason screamed and fell backwards in his chair.

Henry and the dog started laughing.

"Dammit Henry! You scared the hell out of me!"

"Didn't expect to see me, huh?"

"We're you actually listening from outside?"

"Yes."

"Oh… well… have you decided what to do with the circus yet?" Mason asked getting up from the floor.

Henry sat in the chair across from Mason's and picked up his roast beef sandwich. "Well, I went over there today, and I really think they have what it takes to put on a great show if they can just get the right guidance."

And you think you're the one to give them that guidance?"

Henry took the roast beef out from the sandwich.

"That's my lunch. What are you doing?" Mason asked.

Henry threw the roast beef against the wall behind mason and took a bite of the rest. "I do. But I need a small advance first against the money we'll be making to cover the refurbishment costs, and some extra money for my past due rent."

"What money?" Mason asked, looking over at the wad of roast beef stuck to his wall.

"Surely there must be *some* money in the circuses account, right?"

"Yeah, but only enough for them to continue rehearsing for another month or so. After that, it's all over."

"What happens then?"

"Well, you could sell it to the Tingletown Circus. They'd be happy to come in and pick it apart for scrap like they've been trying to do for years. They'll probably also get rid of whatever animals they can't use as well."

Henry's eyes widened like saucers. "Not on my watch they're not!" He quickly shoved the rest of the sandwich into his mouth and stood up forcefully, totally energized. "We can't let that happen, can we!" he shouted enthusiastically, food blasting from his mouth in all directions.

Mason couldn't believe this was actually happening in front of him. He just stood there flinching and trying to keep the food from hitting him in the face. "No sir, but what can you do?"

Henry leaned over, grabbed the roast beef off the wall and tossed it to Fartsnacker who caught it in mid-air. "Leave that to me," Henry said. "I've got an idea that might just do the trick."

The dog barked.

"Also, Fartsnacker says your roast beef is too fatty and it's why those bags under your eyes makes it look like your nose has a saddle. Bye!"

And with that, he and the dog were quickly out the door.

Mason just stood there staring at the doorway, not really sure if he was dreaming or not.

Chapter Six: Banzanos of London

Across town at the Tingletown Circus corporate headquarters, Alexander Tuffington, the large imposing owner of a rival and much better financed mega-circus sat behind his desk, fuming. His henchman Norman Frapp sat across from him.

"So, the old coot's nephew's trying to revive the circus is he?" Tuffington growled.

"Yes sir. We've had his lawyer's office bugged for quite some time now and we just heard they apparently want to keep it all going. They're gonna have quite an uphill battle though. Most of them are total whack snacks, and their trapeze flyer is so huge you could give him an enema and use him as a waterbed."

"I thought when Ballzwick died, that would be the last we'd see of them around here. But now his nephew is seriously trying to bring it all back again?"

"Yes sir, but he's –"

"Not if I can help it!" Tuffington slammed his fist down on the desk. "I want you to do whatever you have to do to shut them down this time. Steal, sabotage, I don't care, just make them go away quickly, and keep it quiet."

"I'll need some help."

"Call those two guys you worked with last time."

"Not them! They were complete morons! They wanted to open a chain of maternity stores called Motherfrockers."

"I don't care. They're loyal and they get the job done. Just call them and keep me posted on everything."

"Yes sir."

Frapp got up from the chair and quickly left the room.

Outside the building on the way to his car, Frapp took out his phone and made a call. "Hey Bunns, this is Frapp. Is your friend still available?... What?... No not single, you dumb sock monkey I want to hire you guys again... Good, be outside the Beacon Street warehouse tomorrow, nine A.M. sharp... Yes, A.M.'s the one in the morning!" He hung up. "Man, I hate when Tuffington makes me work with those idiots!"

# # #

Back over at the circus, everyone was busy rehearsing when Henry and Fartsnacker walked in unseen and quietly walked over to Professor Pottswaller. The Professor smiled when he saw Henry. "Hiya! You here for the gorilla?"

"What gorilla?" Henry asked, totally surprised.

The Professor pointed to Beppi. "That."

Tina heard them and quickly came over. "No daddy, that's Beppi, from the trapeze act."

But the Professor wasn't buying it. "I think he might be a werewolf. There's so much hair on him but he can stand upright."

Tina looked down at Henry's dog. "And who do we have here?"

"Fartsnacker," Henry told her.

"Fartwhat?"

"Snacker."

"You can't be serious!"

"Okay." He then started running all around like a little kid laughing and playing.

"Tina totally cracked up.

Henry ran back to her. "It's a great name for a dog." He looked down at Fartsnacker and scratched its head "He likes it, don't ya boy?"

The dog gave a quick woof.

"See."

"Oh, come on!" Tina said. "He was probably saying 'Why does

29

everyone always laugh at me whenever you call my name?'"

"Not in one woof he couldn't."

"So how did it go at the lawyer's office?"

"It didn't, but that's okay. I've built up enough contacts over the years that if we can get this circus turned around fast enough, I could set up a show for some investors that would get us back in action."

"You really think you can do that?"

"No, but we can sure as hell try, right?"

"Well, it might just work but we'll need to make the show so incredibly entertaining that people won't be able to keep themselves from investing." She turned to the rest of the crowd, "Who's up for the job?"

The clown saluted proudly.

The Banzanos cheered with approval.

The elephant smacked the monkey with its trunk.

The monkey looked at the elephant.

The elephant's pointed at the clown.

# # #

Outside the building, you could hear the clown scream so loud that clusters of birds flew out from many trees.

# # #

Back inside, while Henry and Tina continued making plans, a stagehand in the background pulled the clown out from a basketball hoop.

"So, what's our first move boss?" Tina asked Henry.

"Well, I'd like to see the whole show from start to finish again, that way I can get a better idea of what everyone here can really do when they're not trying to kill each other."

Henry's eye suddenly caught a glimpse of something near the backstage area. "Hey, who's that? I don't remember seeing her before."

Everyone looked over at a sweet older white horse who was

quietly grazing on some hay. She was wearing a pretty blue summer hat with flowers on it and holes cut out for her ears. Tina smiled lovingly at her. "That's Marigold. She's the grande dame of the circus."

They walked over to her. "She was my father's favorite," Tina told him, "And that's saying a lot because he loved all of his animals very much. Marigold and daddy were together for every show they ever did, all the way to the very last one."

Tina pointed to a poster on the wall showing Professor Pottswaller in a dazzling white circus outfit standing in front of a majestic white pony with a beautiful red plume on its head. "People would come from far and wide just to see them perform. They were like magic when they were in the ring together."

Henry quietly pulled over a nearby crate and sat down. Fartsnacker jumped into his lap to hear the story too.

Henry smiled, "Go on."

"Every night at the end of the show, Marigold would stand up on her hind legs so tall and pretty for daddy and the audience. And every time she did that, daddy would give her three sugar cubes to represent three kisses from him."

"Oh my gosh, I think that's the sweetest thing I've ever heard before!" Henry told her.

Tina picked up a nearby brush and gently started brushing Marigold's mane. "They were in the middle of working on a new routine when daddy retired." She pointed up to a large narrow platform high into the air with ramps on both sides leading down to the ground. "Marigold would climb up that narrow ramp on one side, all the way up to the platform where some apples were waiting for her, then she would make her way back down the other side, all while blindfolded."

"How was that possible?" Henry asked. "Wasn't she scared?"

"Never. She just listened to daddy's voice, also there were custom, extra heavy-duty safety harnesses with a slow stop mechanism should anything ever go wrong, which it never did. Plus, she always wore eye shades so she couldn't see how high up she was which wasn't high at all for rehearsals, that way she could get used to her footing. She only went up that platform one time before daddy stopped performing.

"Sounds exhilarating."

"Oh, it was. I just wish I could have seen their last show together. I caught a bad cold and because of it, missed the last time Marigold and daddy were ever in front of an audience together." She put her arms around the horse's neck and hugged her gently. "We still bring her out with us every night in the opening parade, but the last few nights she hasn't been feeling too well so we've been keeping her out to get better. That's why you hadn't seen her before."

Henry gently petted Marigold's neck. "She's beautiful."

"She is indeed. Just wish we could get some of her equipment repaired. It's been a while, and everything is starting to look a bit worn."

"Then let's get this baby up and running! Whattaya say?" Henry asked with a big smile.

Tina smiled right back, walked over to the trapeze rigging and began cranking the safety nets super-tight. She called out to Beppi, "Get up there Bepman and get hooked up! Let's show Henry here why the Banzano family are the greatest flyers in all the world!"

Beppi flashed a huge hairy grin and started hauling his werewolf ass up the ladder as fast as he could, which took a while actually.

Henry grabbed a seat up front and waited for the show to begin.

He looked up... Beppi was still climbing.

And climbing.

Beppi's brother Giuseppe was waiting for him to arrive up on the other platform. "Anytime, fat tits!" Giuseppe shouted.

Beppi, who was still only about halfway there, looked up at his brother. "I'ma gonna keel you when I get upa there!"

"*If*a you get up here, pudding chugger!"

Henry tried to get the attention of Professor Pottswaller who was busy telling the elephant about the importance of sunscreen.

"Just make sure you use at least an SPF 30 or your upper derm will be total crap."

"Hey professor, do you have a minute?" Henry called out.

The professor started quickly rummaging through his pockets then looked back at Henry, "Nope!" He turned back to the elephant, "So anyway..."

Henry just smiled and looked up at Beppi again who was still climbing.

And climbing.

Giuseppe yelled out, "Holy sheet! I shoulda packed a lunch!"

Beppi tried to respond but all he could do was speak gibberish. "Flamma kak pramm!"

"Wow! That'sa some grasp of the English language you got there Tinkerbell!" Giuseppe yelled down with a grin.

The house lights dimmed, and the ringmaster stepped into a single spotlight. "Ladies and gentlemen, children of all ages, please turn your attention to the center ring where we are very proud to bring you, the Dazzling Banzano Flying Trapeze Extravaganza!"

A three-piece band in the corner played a quick *Ta-Da!*

Henry started clapping enthusiastically.

A bright spotlight lit up Beppi... almost there now.

Waiting.

Waiting.

Giuseppe looked at his watch.

With a massive gasp of air, Beppi finally reached the top and blew a big kiss out to the audience. The band played another *Ta-Da!*

Giuseppe rolled his eyes.

The ringmaster continued, "Now let's all watch as the legendary Beppi Banzano attempts the daring Triple Dragon Somersault!"

Beppi cleared his throat loudly and waved his arms erratically at the ringmaster. The ringmaster corrected himself. "Sorry, make that the *Double* Dragon Summersault!"

Beppi waved his arms again and the ringmaster tried once more... "A Summersault!"

Ta da!

Henry lowered his head and pinched the bridge of his nose. "Oh crap."

Giuseppe took hold of the fly bar and swung out across the room to catch Beppi.

The ringmaster continued. "Due to the intense nature of this routine, some of you might want to cover the eyes of your smaller children."

The monkey reached out from behind and covered the clown's eyes. The clown turned around and slapped the monkey.

The monkey kicked the clown in the nuts.

The ringmaster dramatically pointed to Beppi high up in the spotlight. "Watch him if you dare!"

Beppi was now holding the fly bar out in front of him, preparing to swing across to meet Giuseppe.

A drum roll began.

Beppi crossed himself nervously, stepped off the platform and began swinging out towards his brother's waiting arms. He swung out again and again until he was just at the right speed to make the jump.

Henry gulped.

Tina covered her eyes.

The monkey kicked the clown in the nuts again just for fun.

Giuseppe yelled out, "Now, Chunk E. Cheese, now!"

Beppi let go of the bar and sailed out towards his brother.

But out of nowhere, the sound of a donkey braying from down below scared the bejesus out of Beppi and he dropped like a hairy piano right into the net, coming to a slow stop only about ten inches from the ground where he just held there motionless.

Ta da!

Henry lowered his head and pinched the bridge of his nose again. "We're doomed."

The spotlight tilted down to locate the donkey, but it was only Professor Pottswaller on all-fours with snow cone cups for ears, kicking his legs out and braying like a burro. "Hee Haw!!!"

Ta da!

Henry jumped up. "That's it! Turn the lights on!"

Everyone looked over at Henry who was cupping his face in his hands.

Tina walked over. "It's okay, we just have to make sure daddy's tucked away before the performance. It'll be –"

"Look at him!" Henry exclaimed, pointing at Beppi who was still completely motionless in the net, face-down, mustache exploding out between the ropes.

"He didn't even bounce up one time!"

"Okay, so he goes on a diet."

Two stagehands ran over and began trying to remove him from the net.

Beppi began grunting so loudly from the process that it was hard for anyone to continue talking.

Henry tried telling her, "I really don't think he—"

"Uuuuggghhhhh!!!" Beppi blasted out.

"What the hell was that?!" Henry asked both surprised and freaked out.

One of the stagehands tried explaining. "Sorry sir. He's just so big that we can't get all the parts of him out from the net holes fast enough before another hole fills up from somewhere else."

"After I keel my brother, I'ma gonna keel you too keed! Uuugghhppphhhmmmpphh!!!"

"Stop making that sound! It's not natural!" Henry shouted.

The stagehand was losing it. "Oh God, there's so much of him to remove!"

His partner agreed. "I know! The holes just keep filling up out of nowhere!"

"Upa yours you sheety keeds! Uhgrrrrmmmfffff!!!"

Ta da!

Chapter Seven: Who's Weenchops?

Later that night at his apartment, after decompressing from a day he'll never forget, Henry was sitting crisscross applesauce on his spring-exploded couch, looking through a tiny phone book. "I knew there was a reason I hung on to these numbers all these years," he said as he ran his finger down a page in the book. "Ahhh, Madame Gladstone, I think I'll give you a try." He dialed the number, cleared his throat and smiled. "Hello there, is this the enchanting Madame Gladstone? No? Well then who did I call? Weenchops Waxing Paradise! Are you serious? No, I don't want my taint waxed! What? No, I don't care if it's Taintacular Tuesday!" He hung up the phone. "These numbers might be a little out of date." He dialed another one. "Hello, Mr..." he pulled the book up closer to his face, "Buttstash? Am I saying that correctly? Oh, jeez sorry Mr. Beautstagè, I forgot you were French too. Hey, do you know my landlord Mr. Douchebag, he's, hello?" Henry just stared at the phone. "That was rude." He dialed another number. "I hate my life. Oh sorry sir! I didn't expect anyone to answer so quickly. Is this Jimbo Dinkins? It is? Awesome! Hey, this is Henry Sparkleton and hello?" He threw the phone down on the couch cushion. It bounced on the shitty springs and flew all the way over to where DJ Fuzzbuns was lying on floor, scaring the total crap out of the cat. Henry smiled. "DJ, you always know just how to make me feel better."

The cat meowed and started heading down the hall towards the kitchen. Henry yelled after it. "Hey, why would anyone name themselves Jimbo Dinkins anyway?"

The cat meowed noticeably louder this time.

"Yes I know I named you DJ Fuzzbuns, what's your point?!"

The cat meowed again.

"Are you seriously going in there to eat my mustard while giving me shit at the same time?!"

No answer from the cat.

"That's what I thought!"

Henry got up, picked the phone off the floor, plopped back down on the couch and began looking up the next number. "Tim Turde? Are you serious?" He sighed and dialed the number. "This is going to be a lonnnnnng night."

Chapter Eight: Bunns & Alowicious

The next morning across town at an even crappier apartment, Bunns Bazzledoff and Alowicious Purt, both in their twenties and dumber than a bag of wet hammers were playing a video game on a crappy old TV with a rabbit ears antenna.

"Man, this beeping sound is driving me crazy!" Alowicious shouted.

"I know, but this cutting-edge technology stuff is blowing my mind. Admit it, this is totally amazing, right?"

They were playing Pong.

"It *is* amazing. How do they come up with this?" Alowicious asked.

"They probably took wizarding in school." Bunns told him.

Alowicious snapped his finger and pointed at Bunns, "You're right! That's it! That's exactly how they did it. Man, how do you always know just the right answer?"

"Took wizarding in school."

"Oh man! I should have chosen that when I registered!"

"You never registered."

"You know..." he snapped his finger and pointed at Bunns again, "...now that you mention it, that's probably why I never took wizarding, I never thought of that. You're a genius Bunns."

Suddenly a loud knock at the door and both guys instantly dove from their chairs and hit the ground flat at the same time. They looked over at each other and whispered.

"Hey Bunns?"

"Yeah?"

"Why do we always keep falling down here whenever there's a knock at the door?"

"I was just gonna ask you the same thing."

Another knock, this time even louder.

"I think someone's here," Alowicious told him.

"Should we answer it?" Bunns asked.

"Why not," Alowicious answered as he got up and nonchalantly opened the door like nothing happened.

Frapp was standing there fuming. "It's about time you hobo-monkeys answered! What took you so long?" He narrowed his eyes. "You fell on the floor again didn't you?"

They both just looked at each other and answered "No?"

"I told you to be at the warehouse this morning at nine."

"You said AM!" Bunns shouted.

"It is AM!" Frapp yelled back as he pointed to the sky, "The sun's out you thimble-headed dirt squirrels! Get in the car!"

# # #

Back over at the circus, everyone was in the middle of practicing their routines when Tina rallied them all together for an impromptu meeting. "Okay everyone, can I have your attention please?" She looked across the room at her father. "Daddy, the elephant's scrotum is not a hat. Come out from under there please and have a seat up here."

The professor slid out from under the elephant. He was wearing an Elvis jumpsuit, black wig, gold glasses, the whole nine yards. He looked at the elephant. "Hi! How long you been here?"

"Over here daddy," Tina waved.

The professor walked over to her. "Hi! How long you been here?"

"Twenty-four years daddy now sit down by the monkey please and try to listen closely."

The professor took a seat in Beppi's lap.

Beppi just rolled his eyes.

Tina continued. "Now we really need to pull this entire act together for Henry but there's just no way we can keep things the way they are now, so here's my plan..." she looked at Beppi, "... Bepman, you're way too fat. Sorry, you know I love you like family, but you couldn't get off the ground with a rocket up your ass."

Beppi almost choked on his submarine sandwich trying to respond, but Tina nipped it in the bud. "Don't worry though, I've got this whole thing worked out."

Suddenly, a loud a knock at the front door.

"Hold on," she told them. "I'll be right back," then quickly ran from the room.

Beppi just sat there pouting. He looked over at Giuseppe who was grinning at him from ear-to-ear.

Beppi calmly took a piece of paper off a nearby table, scrawled something on it, folded it into a paper airplane and threw it at Giuseppe. It landed in his lap. Giuseppe opened it. *Butt pumpkin.*

Giuseppe just smiled back. "Rocketman."

# # #

Up at the front of the building, Tina opened the door where Bunns and Alowicious were both standing there grinning like idiots.

"Good morning ma'am, allow me to introduce myself. I am Bunns B. Bazzledoff, and this is my esteemed partner Alowicious Pemberton Purt. The reason for our visit here today is because we're doing research for a documentary film about circus life, and we were wondering if we might be able to observe why you all here have lasted in the business as long as you have."

Alowicious stared at Bunns in total disbelief. "Wow, that's the most articulate you've spoken since we've met. You're a really good actor, Bunns!"

Bunns tried to covertly kick him in the shin to get him to shut up.

"Oww! Why'd you kick me?"

Tina, not really sure what was going on, tried to be a good host. "Come on in guys. I can tell you right now though, the reason we've lasted as long as we have is because we treat our animals differently, safer, more compassionately, and we give them love. Lots and lots of love. We just let them do what they want which usually ends up entertaining the crowd much more than anything we could come up with anyway."

She led them into the main room and pointed to a big empty section of bleachers. "You guys can sit anywhere over there you'd like. We should be starting shortly."

"Thank you ma'am, that'll be fine," Bunns told her.

Alowicious looked at him again totally amazed. "When did you start being so polite too?"

"Will you shut up," Bunns whispered forcefully as they walked over to the bleachers and took a couple of seats.

"Well, that wasn't very polite. You sure are fickle," Alowicious told him.

# # #

Over by the performers, Tina hurried back to continue her speech. "So anyways guys, here's the idea I had to get this whole thing fixed up. Ready?... All we need to do is switch the flyer from Beppi, to Granny Whiskers."

"What!?" Beppi and Giuseppe both shouted at the same time.

"I makes the most sense. She weighs only a quarter of what Beppi does, and besides half the time she's so medicated, she'll probably just think she's on a carnival ride or something."

Everyone looked up to the platform at super-thin, boney as hell Granny Whiskers, in a really saggy pink leotard, standing there blowing huge spit bubbles and giggling maniacally when they exploded in her face.

Beppi and Giuseppe looked at each other then turned to Tina, "Could work," they both answered at the same time.

"Damned straight it could!" Henry shouted from the shadows.

Everyone turned around and saw Henry walking up with a big smile on his face.

Tina lit up when she saw him. She liked him.

"Henry! You heard that? You like the idea?"

"I love it. We should start rehearsing it right away. He then noticed the two guys sitting up in the stands. "Who are they?"

41

"They're making a documentary film on circus life. I told them it would be okay if they sat in and watched for a little while. I couldn't see any harm in it."

Henry gave them both a quick once-over, sizin' 'em up. "Well, you can't be too sure. I hear the Tingletown Circus has their beady eyes on this place."

"Oh, they always have, ever since we started taking away their customers. Probably thought they had the market cornered again when Uncle Ballzwick passed away."

"Well, they're about to get even unhappier now because I spent the entire night talking to every investor I know, and between all of them combined, I managed to line up enough money to keep this circus going for another year."

"Henry, that's wonderful!" Tina exclaimed.

"All we need to do," he told her, "is put on a totally flawless, highly entertaining performance for them when they all arrive here to check it out in three days."

"Three days!" Tina exclaimed. "That doesn't give us near as much time as we need. It'd take a miracle to get everything ready by then." Her eyes inadvertently glanced upon a big colorful poster on the wall featuring the entire cast from their glory days, all with happy smiling happy faces. She looked back at Henry, "But I'm sure we can do it. We'll give 'em one hell of a show, I promise you that."

Out in the darkened stands, Bunns and Alowicious had a most concerned look on their faces. "Frapp's not going to like this," Bunns whispered.

"Not one bit," Alowicious agreed.

# # #

Later that night at the Tingletown Circus headquarters, Frapp was sitting across the desk from Tuffington, filling him in on the latest news. "That's what my guys tell me sir. They said they're doing a big show for investors in three days that could save the whole thing if it all went well."

"But it's not going to, is it Frapp?"

"No sir."

"It's not going to go anywhere near well, is it?"

"I'll do my best sir."

Tuffington leaned forward and motioned for Frapp to move in closer as well.

Frapp did.

Tuffington whispered. "Don't make me release the hounds."

Frapp smiled and sat back in his chair, relieved at the joke. "Ah, good one sir. I love that show. I've seen all the episodes multiple times. I've even—"

Tuffington flicked open a lid covering a small red button on his desk and hovered his finger over it. Then suddenly there came the distant wail of angry dogs.

Frapp instantly went into the hard sell. "Not anywhere near well at all sir! Got it! Totally, totally got it!"

Chapter Nine: Preparing for the Big Show

The following morning, Granny Whiskers was rehearsing high up in the air swinging back and forth while hanging on to the bar for dear life and screaming her wrinkled brains out.

Henry, Tina and Beppi were down below trying to keep her calm as she yelled and ranted at them every time she passed over them.

"Come on crazy lady!" Beppi shouted. "You cana do this! Justa like I showed you!"

"I told you, I don't wanna do this, you hairy chimp!" she yelled back.

"It's okay Granny Whiskers!" Henry called out, "Just let go of the bar when you hear Beppi yell *now*, okay?"

"Upa yours, vacuum boy!"

"Don't worry granny," Tina shouted, "there's a net underneath you, so there's nothing to fear at all!"

"I'ma gonna pee!" she yelled.

"That's okay! That's what I do!" Beppi yelled back. "Justa let it go and enjoy the ride!"

Everyone looked over at Beppi, especially Giuseppe. "I'ma never catching you again, dirtbag!"

"See! I alwaysa told you, you were a dirtbag!" Granny shouted from above.

Suddenly another loud knock at the door surprised them all.

"I'll go see who that is," Henry told everyone. "Keep working with Granny and I'll be right back." He did a quick jog to the front room and was out of sight.

Beppi looked up at Granny Whiskers and smiled. "Okay Fu Manchu, let'sa do this!"

# # #

In the front room, Henry opened the door and Bunns and Alowicious were once again standing there smiling like goobers.

"Good morning! I'm Bunns and this is Alowicious. We're here to —"

"And I'm Henry! Congratulations on those names! See ya later, urinal cakes!" he said slamming the door loudly in their faces. He just stood there for a moment with a satisfied smile. "Man, that slam felt good being on the other side for a change."

Outside, the two guys just looked at each other totally confused.

"Well, what are we supposed to do now?" Alowicious asked.

"I dunno. Our ride's gone so we're kinda stuck here."

"Wait, no we're not! I can move!" Alowicious said excitedly as he started lifting his feet up and down.

"Hey, I got it," Bunns told him, "We'll knock on the door again and tell him we left something here yesterday and need to pick it up."

"Good idea. What's something a film crew would leave behind?"

"A camera?"

"No."

"Film?"

"No."

"Despair?"

"Yeah!" Alowicious shouted. "Let's use that!"

They knocked on the door again. Henry answered immediately just like nothing had happened. "Come on in guys! Happy to see you! I'll show you to your seats."

They both stepped inside totally confused again, but dutifully followed Henry as he guided them into the main room. "We're rehearsing for an important show today and need to get everything just right," Henry told them.

Alowicious tried to pump him for info along the way. "Yes,

umm, could you tell us more about that important show please?" He looked over at Bunns and flicked his eyebrows up and down.

"It's a very special show we're doing for some investors who could save us from bankruptcy," Henry told them.

"Really? Do tell," Alowicious asked, flicking his eyebrows up and down again at Bunns.

Henry wasn't sure why he was doing that. "Well, the person who this circus was named after, my uncle Ballzwick Sparkleton, passed away recently and left the circus to—"

"His nephew?" Alowicious interrupted like he was some great detective. His eyebrows were really going off now too.

Henry couldn't take it any longer. "Hey, what the hell's wrong with those eyebrows? It's like they're trying to jump off your face or something! Is that a medical condition? If not... stop it! It's freaking me out!" He pointed to some bleachers, "Go sit over there."

Henry quickly walked off into the darkness, leaving Bunns and Alowicious standing there looking more confused than ever.

"What just happened?" Alowicious asked.

"I have no idea, but let's get on with why we're here."

"Good idea," Alowicious agreed. "Why are we here?"

Bunns reached into his jacket pocket and pulled out a tiny bottle. "Here's the stuff Frapp gave us to use," He handed it to Alowicious. "That's fart sauce for the monkey. Gives it gas *real* bad. Doesn't hurt him at all but makes it blow ass like you've never heard in your life."

"Sweet! What's next?"

Bunns pulled out another small bottle. "This one's for the elephant."

"What's it do?"

"Makes it sneeze like a nuclear-powered t-shirt gun."

"Oh man, this is gonna be so much fun!" Alowicious giggled as he quietly jumped up and down.

"But wait dipshit... there's more," Bunns whispered with a smile. He pulled out one more bottle from his coat. "Last but not least... one for the dwarf." He rotated it around so that Alowicious could read the entire label: *PURE CAROLINA REAPER OIL. SCOVILLE RATING 2,200,000. EXTREME CAUTION MANDATORY - MAY CAUSE COLON TO UNLODGE!*

"I'm adding it to the water the clown uses in his dripping umbrella routine. You know, the one he carries out and sprays into the audience?"

"How delightfully dastardly," Alowicious said with a malicious grin.

"Frapp had the other two elixirs made so they'd take effect in forty-eight hours from the time ingested, which should make that just about perfect for show time."

"You are a wicked, wicked man, and also my idol," Alowicious told him. "Come on, let's hurry up and get back home so we can play more of that mind-blowing beeping game on TV."

Bunns lit up with a big smile. "I'm with ya there pal!"

The two guys headed happily off in different directions to do their evil deeds, while backstage, Tina was just finishing talking with her father.

"So daddy, when you eat pickles, you don't have to put your entire head inside the jar, you can just take one out at a time with your fingers, okay?"

The professor smiled sweetly and nodded. She lifted his hat and kissed him on the head again.

Henry was just walking up from behind. "Excuse me, if you're giving out kisses, could you tell me where the line starts please?"

Tina giggled.

"No?" Henry said. "Well then could you tell me what *this* is for?" He held out his hand with a tiny camera sitting in the palm of it.

Tina looked at it and laughed. "Oh, that was a great idea Uncle Ballzwick had where we attached little cameras to the top of the animal's heads to give the audience their perspective of the show. We'd then put it up on a big screen during the performance for the whole audience to see."

"Sounds great, can we have it ready for the show?"

"I actually just had the stagehands wire up the cameras earlier today, so all that's left for us to do is get the screen set up."

"Then I'll help you with that right now. Where is it?"

Tina pointed to several large crates across the room. "Should be in one of those over there."

"Thanks," Henry said as he quickly headed over to them.

Along the way, he unknowingly passed by Alowicious who was hiding behind some boxes near the monkey's food bowl. After Henry had completely passed by, Alowicious unscrewed the bottle of fart sauce, poured it all over the monkey's food, then smiled most dastardly. "The butthorn on that monkey will have completely jumped off its body in total desperation by the time this stuff wears off," he said giggling as he slithered away into the darkness.

Across the other side of the room, Bunns was by the elephant's dish, unscrewing the lid from the sneeze juice. He poured half the bottle into the elephant's water bowl, then looked around at all the empty seats. "The people in those seats are gonna need raincoats for their raincoats when this stuff kicks in," he said smiling... then poured the other half into the bowl just for good measure. "Or a boat," he said breaking into quiet laughter as he too slipped away into the darkness and out of sight.

Chapter Ten: It's Pucker Time!

Circus time had arrived, and the Amazing Sparkleton Circus was primed and ready for the biggest performance of its life! Bright, colorful balloons were tied to the backs of all the bleachers, glitter and confetti shimmered everywhere, and sparkling banners filled the room all around.

Backstage, Henry had rallied the troops together. Fartsnacker was there too, even DJ Fuzzbuns was on hand with his very own bag of mustard-covered peanuts.

"Okay guys this is it!" Henry told them. "The audience out there tonight is filled with both local townsfolk and out-of-town investors alike, and they're all here to have one of the greatest nights of their life, so whattaya say we give it to 'em?"

The entire cast cheered excitedly.

Henry continued. "And are they gonna tell all their friends about tonight?"

"Yeah!!!" they shouted in unison.

"And are they all gonna remember this night for as long as they live?"

"Yeah!!!"

"And are they gonna... Professor, you wanna take your finger out from that lady's ear please."

Professor Pottswaller was standing in the front row smiling like a cute little bald whacksnack with his finger in some random woman's ear. The lady was really uncomfortable too and just stared straight ahead, not really sure if it was part of the show or not.

The professor, wearing speedos, a snorkel, and diving flippers, kissed the lady's nose and pulled his finger out from her ear with a squeaky pop, then casually walked over to join the rest of the cast.

The lady just sat there looking totally confused.

"Thank you professor," Henry told him. "You can grab a seat over there by the monkey."

The professor sat in Beppi's lap again.

Beppi got ready to say something, but the professor just kissed him on the nose too.

Totally disarmed, Beppi could only smile back sweetly.

# # #

At the entrance of the circus, Tuffington, Frapp, Bunns and Alowicious discreetly walked inside the room with the rest of the crowd and quietly took some seats towards the back. They looked at each other and smiled confidently.

# # #

Backstage, Henry was just finishing up with his pep talk. "Now I know all of you have worked really hard these last..." he noticed Granny Whiskers tying little ribbons onto each side of her long mustache, "...few days to get this show to where we are tonight, so let's get out there and give these people a night they'll remember forever!"

# # #

In the audience, Frapp leaned over to Tuffington. "I do believe sir this will be a night we'll remember forever."

Tuffington smiled and nodded in agreement... just as the lights went out.

The crowd began to applaud with excitement and the band started to play. The show had begun.

A single spotlight illuminated the Ringmaster. "Good evening ladies and gentlemen, boys and girls of all ages! Welcome to a night of pure magic! Welcome... to the Amazing Sparkleton Circus!"

The crowd erupted with cheer.

A second spotlight came on and illuminated a happy smiling clown who was just walking out amongst the audience carrying a big umbrella.

"Looks like we've got some company here with us tonight folks!" The ringmaster continued. "Say hello to Crumpet, our Mighty Mini Clown!"

The crowd applauded enthusiastically.

Alowicious looked over at Frapp and flicked his eyebrows up and down.

Frapp hates it when he does that. "Stop it moron."

"Hey Crumpet," the ringmaster called out, "do you think it's gonna rain tonight?"

Crumpet held out his palm to feel for rain and nodded yes. He began opening his umbrella.

The audience giggled with anticipation.

Bunns and Alowicious' eyes widened like saucers.

And with much fanfare, the clown raised up the umbrella, quickly snapped it open… and… nothing happened.

A man directly underneath the umbrella looked straight up at it.

Still nothing.

The clown began shaking the handle hard trying to get it to work.

It didn't.

He lifted the umbrella up and looked underneath it.

Bunns turned to Frapp. "Sorry boss, I don't know what happened. It was supposed to –"

The clown's super-high-pitched shriek suddenly shattered all other noises in the room as he began running around uncontrollably, screaming his tiny nuts off and ramming into everyone's legs like a pinball machine. It was awesome.

Everyone in the audience was straining like crazy to see what was going on.

Apparently a clog in the umbrella had finally broken loose and soaked the little guy down, making him run blindly throughout the crowd, banging into everything while also tripping over chairs and swearing like crazy.

The audience thinks it's part of the show and totally loved it. They cheered wildly at the spectacle.

The ringmaster doesn't know what to do next though, so he covered the microphone and leaned over to Henry who was standing nearby in the shadows. "What's up with the clown?"

"I don't know, but it worked. Just move on to the Banzanos and I'll go make sure he's okay."

The ringmaster nodded and continued with the show. "Ladies and gentlemen, please turn your attention toward the heavens and delight at the wonderous spectacle of the Banzano Family Trapeze Extravaganza!"

The audience cheered.

A single spotlight moved across the room and illuminated the high platform where Beppi was sitting in a chair, hunched over and pouting like crazy, while Granny Whiskers stood next to him flipping off Giuseppe who was swinging back and forth on the bar waiting to catch her.

"Watch as Mama Banzano prepares to fly through the air with extreme precision."

Henry started chanting over and over. "Please just don't ask her how she's doing. Please just don't ask her how she's doing. Please don't ask her –"

"How are you doing up there, Mama Banzano?"

"Blow it out your puckered starfish you radio putz, get me the hell down from here!"

"Oh crap," Henry exclaimed as he bolted for the microphone, yanked it from Fred's hands and took over the show. "Let's hear it ladies and gentlemen for our new comedy sensation, the Amazing Ballzwick Players!"

Everyone cheered with approval.

Tina peeked around from behind the curtain and gave Henry a big thumbs-up.

He smiled with relief. "Now it's time to bring out our fabulous animal stars! Whattaya say everyone?"

The audience loved it.

A bright spotlight lit up the main curtain behind Henry and a loud drum roll began.

"Ladies and gentlemen, the Amazing Sparkleton Circus is now proud to bring you some of the smartest animals on the planet. And leading their way, will be none other than their loving, and may I say exceptionally beautiful trainer, Tina Pottswaller!"

The curtain behind him opened up and out walked Tina, with Chester the monkey close at hand.

The audience applauded happily.

Chester was pulling a big red wagon behind him with a dog riding in it. They all began circling the room for everyone to see.

The monkey waved to the audience while the dog began doing back-flips in the wagon.

The audience cheered even louder.

"What do you think everyone? Aren't they adorable?"

A huge blast of air from the monkey's ass suddenly made him stop walking and just look back at its butt for a moment.

"And that's Chester the monkey who's happy to see you all! Chester, say 'Hi' to all the beautiful folks out there tonight!"

PHFFFFFFFFRRRRRRRP!

A kaiju fart blasted from monkey bung with extreme force, making the monkey jump forward several feet. Totally surprised, it quickly looked behind it again.

PHFFFFFFFFRRRRRRRP!

He jumped ahead once more, not sure what the hell was going on.

PHFFFFFFFFRRRRRRRP!

Now he realized he was only farting uncontrollably and decided to just enjoy it. He bent over and really started workin' 'em down.

PHFFFFFFFFRRRRRRRP!   *PHFFFFFFFFRRRRRRRP!*
PHFFFFFFFFRRRRRRRP!

The audience exploded with laughter.

The dog behind him wasn't laughing at all though since it was taking the full brunt of the farts. It just jumped out of the wagon and tore off running backstage yelping like crazy.

The audience was in hysterics.

The monkey started laughing too. *PHFFFFFFFFRRRRRRRP! PHFFFFFFFFRRRRRRRP! PHFFFFFFFFRRRRRRRP!*

Tuffington glared at Frapp, "They're loving this! This isn't what I paid you for!" He slapped Frapp on the back of his head. So Frapp slapped Bunns who slapped Alowicious who slapped the lady sitting next to him.

From way across the room, Alowicious could be seen flying high up into the air from the woman's punch, then crashing back down into his chair.

Henry leaned over to Tina. "What the hell's going on around here?"

"I don't know, but this is the weirdest show we've ever had."

Henry motioned for Fred to come back and take over the mic again.

Fred giggled with excitement and quickly ran back up. Henry smiled and handed him the mic. "Okay baby, bring it on home."

Fred clutched the mic tightly in his hand, grinned like a Cheshire cat, sucked in a deep breath, then faced the crowd. "Ladies and gentlemen, let's circus this mother down!"

The crowd went wild.

A spotlight lit up the curtain behind him, it opened wide and out proudly walked Pagoda the elephant. It was a massive, beautiful animal, wearing a sparkling red and gold circus banner draped over its immense frame. It was walking alongside Wildfire the horse and together they circled the ring one time then came to a stop next to Tina and the monkey.

PHFFFFFFFFRRRRRRRP!

Tina, the horse, and the elephant all looked at the monkey.

PHFFFFFFFFRRRRRRRP! PHFFFFFFFFRRRRRRRP!

The audience could not stop laughing.

Neither could the monkey. It looked at the elephant and flicked its eyebrows up and down.

The elephant swung its trunk out to smack the monkey into the next time zone, but it suddenly stopped and began to sniffle. Just a little at first, but soon it was sucking in a ginormous breath.

The monkey could care less though, he was having a blast.

Literally. He clasped both hands high up into the air like he was winding up for a big baseball pitch.

The elephant was still sucking in a massive breath.

The monkey thinks it's because of him, so he quickly stuck its butt out right at the elephant for another nice rip, but from out of nowhere, Fred walked over and stopped directly in-between them. "Isn't she a beautiful animal folks? Watch as Pagoda, the Elephant of Wonder makes –"

That's all Fred could get out before a bucket-size sneeze of elephant snot blasted out all over him, sending his hairpiece eight rows back into the audience. It finally came to rest in some lady's lap who to this very day is still screaming uncontrollably.

The audience was peeing in their pants.

The elephant took in another huge breath, turned directly towards the monkey, and this time blasted out a righteous snot rocket right at it, completely soaking the thing down from head-to-toe.

The monkey just stood there in total shock, holding its dripping arms straight out away from its sides... and farting uncontrollably.

Tina quickly took hold of the elephant and walked it away from the monkey, which inadvertently brought the elephant even closer to the audience... the first rows of which were filled with really old ladies on a field trip. Henry was right about karma.

The elephant sucked in another monstrous breath as it moved even closer towards the audience.

An exceptionally old lady in the front row looked at the elephant. "That's the ugliest dog I've ever seen before!"

The elephant turned its head right towards her and immediately horked out a gargantuan sneeze, glazing her face down with pachyderm punch.

The entire audience was now rolling in the aisles with laughter...Well, all except for the old lady and Tuffington.

Henry was just trying to figure out what to do next when a stagehand, holding one of the tiny cameras in his hand came out from the backstage area and walked up to him. "Excuse me sir, but you know these camera's I was told to rig up for the animals earlier?"

"Not personally, we've only spoken once or twice."

"Well, before the show I had the cameras turned on a while to do a test run on everything."

"How very thoughtful of you. Please continue."

"Well, the cameras picked up something else other than just the rehearsals. Take a look."

Henry looked into the little remote screen on the camera and his eyes widened. He grabbed the camera, ran over to the audio-visual control panel, plugged it in and pushed a button. The big screen on stage instantly lit up for all to see. It showed the monkey's point-of-view as he was playing with an assortment of rubber balls.

The audience hushed and watched with delight.

The monkey casually picked up one of the rubber balls and threw it at the clown like it always does, nailing the clown in the back of the head. The impact made the clown trip over a water bowl and crash into some nearby boxes.

The audience cracked up again.

On screen, Tina could be seen running over and helping the clown back to his feet. She then walked over to the monkey, removed the camera from its head, placed it on a stack of nearby crates, then gently took the monkey's arm and guided it away backstage. After a moment, Bunns and Alowicious walked up to the crates and stood next to them. Their voices were picked up very clearly by the little camera.

"Look, here's the stuff Frapp gave us to use," Bunns told Alowicious.

He handed him a tiny bottle. "That's fart sauce for the monkey. Gives it gas *real* bad. Doesn't hurt him at all but makes it blow ass like you've never heard in your life."

"Sweet! What's next?"

In the audience, Bunns and Alowicious were starting to sweat something insane, sitting there with their mouths wide open, staring at the screen in utter disbelief while Frapp and Tuffington glared at them both unmercifully.

On the screen, Bunns was continuing. "This one's for the elephant."

"What's it do?"

"Makes it sneeze like a nuclear-powered t-shirt gun."

"Oh man, this is gonna be so much fun!"

"But wait dipshit... there's more... last but not least... one for the dwarf. I'm adding it to the water he uses in his dripping umbrella routine. You know, the one he carries out and sprays into the audience?"

A loud voice from the real backstage was suddenly heard. It was the clown.

"Asshole!!!"

The footage suddenly came to an end.

The house lights turned on and Henry was standing off to the side of the control panel pointing up to Tuffington in the crowd. "Is there a police officer in the house that can go up there and arrest those men?"

All eyes instantly turned to Tuffington who was still glaring at his three men like he wanted to kill every one of them.

Bunns, Alowicious, and Frapp just slide down in their seats.

Henry called out to Tuffington. "So Tuffington, I assume those men work for you?"

Alowicious jumped up, pointed to Tuffington and shouted. "We've never seen that man before in our lives!"

Nobody was buying it.

"Okay, maybe we've seen him before, but he scares me really bad and spits food through his teeth when he yells at me!"

Tuffington jumped up from his seat and tried strangling Bunns and Alowicious at the same time. They both screamed like he was trying to take away their pong.

Three security guards immediately arrived and pulled Tuffington off of them.

Once, and only once Tuffington had been completely subdued, Bunns stomped his foot down really hard and forcefully pointed at Tuffington. "Oh, that's it buddy! You really did it this time!

You're lucky I don't come over there and –"

Tuffington yanked himself away from the grasp of the security guards and leapt at Bunns.

Bunns' scream was so high that Fartsnacker and Fuzzbuns instantly ran from the room to shield their ears.

Two more security guards, along with an off-duty police officer quickly arrived and pulled Tuffington away from Bunns.

The police officer handcuffed Tuffington, while the security guards handcuffed the other three and began leading them away.

Bunns leaned over to Tuffington as they walked. "Sorry about the whole 'oh that's it buddy' thing. You're a powerful and scary man and I would never have said that if I –"

Tuffington cut him off and narrowed his eyes, "I'm going to erase you and your idiot friend from this entire planet if it's the last thing I do. Do you understand me... buddy?"

Bunns just blinked at him in complete shock for a few moments, then very slowly began to cry. Only a few sniffles at first, but then quickly turning into full-blown sobs.

Alowicious tried to console him. "Hey, look at it this way, we'll both be heroes when we introduce everyone in prison to that cool new beeping game on TV we discovered."

Frapp leaned over to him. "Neither of you will ever live to make it that far."

Alowicious slowly began to cry himself now, then together, both he and Bunns could be heard wailing loudly all the way out the building.

Henry quickly grabbed the microphone. "Ladies and gentlemen, I can assure you that this would never have happened if –"

A loud voice from the audience immediately interrupted him. "I do believe we've all seen just about enough, Mr. Sparkleton!"

All eyes in the room quickly turned towards the voice.

Henry lowered his head and pinched the bridge of his nose. "Oh crap."

Out from the shadows of the audience, a figure stood up and started making its way through the rows of people... heading straight for Henry.

"Oh crap," Henry said again.

The figure reached the bottom of the rows and began stepping out into the ring and into the light.

Henry shaded the spotlight over his eyes to better see who it was. "Mr. Buttstash?" he asked completely surprised.

"That's Beautstagè, Sparkleton. I'm French, remember?"

"Yeah, but Buttstash is much funnier."

The man walked up and slapped Henry hard on the shoulder, scaring the crap out of him.

"Henry?" the man called out.

"Yes?" Henry said jumping a foot in the air. "Don't hurt me."

"You did your uncle proud!"

"What?"

"That old medicine man, your uncle was my best friend when we were kids. He used to put on magic shows for us kids in elementary school during lunch and make Tommy Turdwheeler shoot milk from his nose from all the jokes he would tell."

"Tommy Whatwheeler? Wait, hold on, I think buttstash may have just been dethroned!"

Beautstagè smiled and put his arm around Henry. "Who'd of thought the guy I bought my vacuum cleaner from was the nephew of my childhood pal."

"Was his name *really* Turdwheeler?"

"Listen kid, I like the charm of this circus and I like how you handled everything tonight. Things could have gotten a lot worse, but you and your gang pulled it off marvelously."

"We gotta name the clown Turdwheeler!"

"Forget the name kid! I'm trying to have a special moment here!"

Henry looked over at the cast who were now all standing around him smiling. He smiled back at them with love in his eyes.

Mr. Beautstagè continued. "You all are just the kind of thing I'd trust my money to be fruitful with and multiply." He smiled and winked at Henry. "I've got lots of it too."

Henry's face lit up big-time. He scooped up Mr. Beautstagè and swung him around the room, almost nailing the dwarf which coincidentally the monkey was actually off to the side praying for.

Henry put him back down. "Sorry, I'm a hugger. I just thought that –"

A women's horrifying scream cut through the celebration.

All eyes quickly turned to a woman in the audience pointing up to Marigold the old horse, who'd been slowly walking up the high narrow ramp in the dark, with no harness and no safety net.

The audience gasped.

Tina was shocked. "Marigold! Stay!" she called out.

The horse stopped and looked down at Tina.

"Don't move Marigold! Stay right there!"

The horse, looking sweet and somber, only turned away and continued walking up towards the top.

"Oh God no, please."

Some of the audience began to scream.

Henry rushed over to Tina. "Why is she doing that?"

"I think she wants to perform one last time like she remembered rehearsing with daddy."

"But she's supposed to have safety equipment and a net."

"I know that, but Marigold doesn't remember."

Tina desperately called out to the horse again. "Marigold, stay girl!"

The horse slowed down just a bit, but after a moment it continued towards the top.

Tina was now panicking. "Henry, I don't know how to make her stop. She'll fall!"

"I'll try running up the other side of the ramp. You go to the –"

"Stay baby!" A familiar voice called out.

Marigold froze in her tracks.

The spotlight and all eyes moved down to Professor Pottswaller who was standing there in his classic white circus outfit and holding his arms straight up towards the horse.

A hush ran through the crowd.

The professor smiled warmly at Marigold. "It's me baby. Everything's going to be okay."

The sweet horse seemed to recognize her old friend.

"I'm here to help you sweetheart."

But the horse thinks the only way down is forward, so she takes another step.

The crowd gasps again.

"Stay Marigold! Don't move! Listen! Remember the last trick we were working on?"

The horse shifted its head curiously.

"Think Marigold! The one where you walk backwards then stand up pretty for the crowd?"

Marigold took another step forward.

"No Marigold! Backwards! Listen baby!"

The professor walked to the end of the ramp Marigold had walked up on.

"I'm right behind you sweetheart, listen to the sound of my voice, just like I taught you.

The horse doesn't do anything.

You could hear a pin drop.

"Backwards baby. Towards my voice."

The horse is completely still.

"My voice Marigold! Backwards to my voice!"

Slowly, the horse began to take a step backwards.

Tense murmurs rumbled throughout the audience.

"Good girl Marigold! Good girl! Another step baby, straight backwards!"

She took another step.

"That's it! Now another! Towards my voice!"

Marigold took another step, then another and another.

The crowd slowly began to clap.

"That's my good girl Marigold!"

Marigold took another step but a little too far to the left and one of her legs slipped off.

The audience screamed in terror.

The professor though, remained cool as a cucumber. "Marigold, center girl, center."

After a quick muscle shift, the horse stood up and regained her footing.

"Good girl! Just like I taught you now, towards my voice!"

Marigold slowly took another step backyards, then another and another, until she suddenly found her inner center and confidently began walking backwards down the ramp faster and more perfectly with each step she took.

The audience began to cheer louder and louder.

"That's it baby! You're doing it, you're doing it!"

And when the horse had finally reached the very bottom, Professor Pottswaller walked up and gave her the biggest hug she'd ever known.

The audience were on their feet, cheering with all their might.

A stagehand came over with Marigold's beautiful red feather plume and gently placed it on top of her head.

Then with his arms held lovingly around her neck, the professor whispered into Marigold's ear. "Ready for the big finish girl? Just you and me?"

The horse nuzzled its head in close to the professor.

"Then let's sit prettier than anyone has ever seen before in their lives... for the very last time my beautiful girl."

The professor's tears could be seen reflecting in the big brown eyes of the horse. She gently rubbed her head against his.

"I've missed you very much Marigold." He then kissed her head, took a step backwards, bolstered himself proudly and raised one arm high up into the air. And as he did, Marigold, just like she was still a mare, sat up so high and grand on both her hind legs that it literally took the breath away of many who were there that night to witness it.

The entire building erupted with cheer, the likes of which no one had ever heard before. Two cannons filled with sparkling circus ribbons shot high up all around them, filling the entire room with color and excitement.

The professor put his hand in his pocket and pulled out three sugar cubes.

Tina saw them and began to cry.

Marigold looked down and saw the sugar cubes in his hand. She then looked up at the professor and her eyes sparkled warmly. She lowered her head back down and gently took the three kisses from his hand.

The professor put his arms around her neck again and whispered to her once more. "Listen to that crowd. You're the biggest star here tonight Marigold."

The horse was in heaven. Warm and safe in her old friend's arms once again, and with the audience cheering for her like they used to long ago.

"I'm going to need to go soon Marigold, but always remember that I love you. I love you so very much, and I always will."

Tina was bawling as she and Henry walked over to them.

"Daddy, what happened? How are you able to be here so clearly for so long?"

The professor just looked at her and smiled. "Both my girls needed me."

Tina beamed. She put her arms around her daddy and hugged him so close. She then grabbed Marigold and hugged her tightly as well.

A single feather drifted down from Marigold's red plume and fell softly to the ground. It came to rest near a cluster of sparkling circus ribbons from the cannon.

"*That's* where the red feather and ribbons in my shoebox came from!" Henry exclaimed. The white horse in that picture with me was Marigold." He smiled at Tina. "I was there! I saw them in their heyday!" And then, with the bliss of a child, Henry grabbed the microphone from Fred's hand and proudly announced to the entire audience… "Ladies and gentlemen, it is with the greatest of pleasure and most humble of tidings that I present to you on this very special evening, the one, the only, the Amazing Sparkleton Circus!"

The crowd exploded with cheer.

Beppi, Giuseppe, Granny Whiskers, Hugo the clown, Tina and Professor Pottswaller all looked at each other and smiled proudly.

Tina leaned over and gave Henry a sweet kiss on his cheek.

The monkey leaned over and gave the clown bunny ears.

The professor leaned over and whispered into Beppi's ear. "Hey, isn't it true a bigamist is just a fog over Italy?"

Beppi smiled and whispered back. "Ima gonna keel you fruitcake."

"Catch me if you can Stromboli."

Then with a shot, the professor took off running with Beppi following right behind, albeit at a much, much, much slower pace.

Ta da!

Manufactured by Amazon.ca
Bolton, ON

44311014R00037